WELCOME TO
MAYBERRY
The Friendly Town

I'm Proud to Call You My Friend

A COLLECTION OF SPECIAL MOMENTS OF FRIENDSHIP FROM *THE ANDY GRIFFITH SHOW*

Compiled by Ken Beck and Jim Clark

RUTLEDGE HILL PRESS™ • NASHVILLE, TENNESSEE
A DIVISION OF THOMAS NELSON, INC.
www.ThomasNelson.com

Dedicated to the cast, production crew, and writers of
The Andy Griffith Show

The Andy Griffith Show and all related elements TM & © 2002 by Mayberry Enterprises, Inc.
All Rights Reserved.

Additional material and compilation copyright © 2002 Ken Beck & Jim Clark

Published by Rutledge Hill Press, a Thomas Nelson company,
P.O. Box 141000, Nashville, Tennessee 37214.

Design by OneWomanShow Design, Franklin, TN.

Photos on pages 11, 14, 14, and 30 are courtesy of Gilmore-Schwenke Archives.
Background photo on page 64 is courtesy of Joel Rasmussen Collection.

Library of Congress Cataloging-in-Publication Data

I'm proud to call you my friend: a collection of special moments from
the Andy Griffith show / compiled by Ken Beck and Jim Clark.
     p. cm.
   ISBN 1-55853-994-8 (hardcover)
   1. Andy Griffith show (Television program) I. Beck, Ken, 1951- II.
Clark, Jim, 1960-
   PN1992.77.A573 I5 2002
   791. 45'72--dc21

                                              2002003735

Printed in the United States of America

02 03 04 05 06—5 4 3 2 1

Acknowledgments

We had a lot of help from good friends in putting together this book. At Rutledge Hill Press, publisher Larry Stone has always supported our interest in Mayberry, as have Bryan Curtis and editor Geoff Stone and all of the Rutledge Hill team.

We also have special thanks for designer Angie Jones, whose graphics work for this book captured the spirit of Mayberry and helped make the friends and words that we're familiar with seeing and hearing on television come to life on paper as well.

We thank the good folks at Viacom for their efforts in licensing this book. In particular, we thank Risa Kessler and Phyllis Ungerleider.

For assistance with gathering photographs, we thank Jason Gilmore and Jim Schwenke of Gilmore-Schwenke Archives, Bart Boatwright, Joel Rasmussen, and TAGSRWC Archives. We're especially grateful to Allan Newsome for his help with supplying images. And we thank the actors whose characters are pictured in this book. They are the people who made us truly love the characters, their words, and Mayberry itself.

Credit for most of the words (and all of the important ones!) in this book goes to the extraordinary writers who worked on The Andy Griffith Show. They were the best in the business. Their credits appear with their words throughout the book.

Ken thanks his wife, Wendy, and daughter Kylie and son Cole. Jim thanks his wife, Mary. All have been best friends during our continuing devotion to Mayberry.

And finally, our ultimate thanks go to Andy Griffith, who is simply the best friend Mayberry will ever have. Period.

Introduction

If ever a place has stood for friendliness, it has to be Mayberry. As Andy Taylor himself once said, "Ain't we lucky to live in such a friendly town!"

Whether in Mayberry or somewhere else, friendships are something everyone is fortunate to have and would be wise to maintain because friends are treasures that are difficult to replace.

In this little book, we highlight, in words and pictures, some of the special moments of friendship among the characters of The Andy Griffith Show—*the TV friends of millions of loyal fans. Some of the instances are simply one line of commentary. Others are more extensive dialogue among characters. Some of the captured moments are poignant, others just humorous. But they all demonstrate some of the many dimensions of friendship in Mayberry and, by reflection and extension, the world beyond it.*

As part of our way of extending the benefits of Mayberry, a portion of the proceeds from the sale of this book is being donated to the Surry Arts Council in Andy Griffith's hometown of Mount Airy, North Carolina. Among its many community efforts, the Surry Arts Council organizes the Mayberry Days festival that is held in Mount Airy each September.

In any case, maybe you will discover something thought-provoking about friendship as you read this book. Or perhaps you'll find an occasion to laugh as you are reminded of a particular funny scene. At the very least, we hope you enjoy a nice visit with some favorite friends.

Meanwhile, when you see friends, tell 'em, "Goober says hey!"

—K.B. and J.C.

WARREN FERGUSON (to Andy):

I'm proud to call you my friend.

"The Bazaar," Episode 164
Written by Ben Joelson and Art Baer

Being a friend sometimes means realizing that rules are made to serve people and not the other way around, as when new pharmacist Ellie Walker eventually decides to give ailing old Emma Brand some pills that she badly wants:

ELLIE: I'm a pharmacist and there are certain prescribed rules I'm sworn to follow.

ANDY: Well, I know. And that's good. I mean, rules and different things like that are fine things to have, I reckon. But sometimes, well, every once in a while, you have to think of the folks involved in it—like Emma getting sick because she didn't have them pills. What do they call it in the books? I believe—what is it?—

the human equation, I think it is.

You must believe that, too, or you wouldn't have brought 'em to her.

"Ellie Comes to Town," Episode 4
Written by Charles Stewart and Jack Elinson

ANDY (to Opie): When you make a promise to a friend, it ain't right to go back on it. No.

Never let your friend down,

never break a trust, and

when you give your word,

never go back on it."

"Runaway Kid," Episode 6
Written by Arthur Stander

When Andy finds out that hometown success story Jim Lindsey wasn't so prosperous and famous after all, Jim learns that true friendship isn't changed by degrees of success:

ANDY: What did you put on such a big act for?

JIM: What did you expect me to do? Come back to my own hometown and say, "Come on, folks. Come look at your hometown failure."

ANDY: I think you're kinda underestimating your friends a little.

JIM: What do you mean?

ANDY: Waddn't you treated pretty good before you left? And you waddn't a big star nor nothin'. **Why should folks think any less of you now?**

"The Guitar Player Returns," Episode 31
Written by Charles Stewart and Jack Elinson

BARNEY (to Thelma Lou): I'm sure of it. This Rogers is obviously a better qualified man. He makes a better deputy. No, I'm a fifth wheel and I know it.

THELMA LOU: Then why wouldn't Andy say something to you?

BARNEY: Well, that's the worst of it—the waiting. Why doesn't he just come out and say, "Barney, you're through."

THELMA LOU: Oh, I don't care what you say, Barney.

Andy's too good a friend to ever tell you you're through.

BARNEY: Well, sure he's a friend. I know that, but hey, that's why he hasn't said anything. He *is* a friend. He don't know how to fire me. He can't find the words. Well, maybe I can do something about that. Maybe I'll just find the words for him.

THELMA LOU: Barney, what do you mean?

BARNEY: Well, I'll make it easy for him. Barney Fife isn't wanted someplace, Barney Fife doesn't stay. I'll just bow out.

"Barney's Replacement," Episode 34
Written by Jack Elinson and Charles Stewart

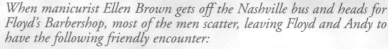

When manicurist Ellen Brown gets off the Nashville bus and heads for Floyd's Barbershop, most of the men scatter, leaving Floyd and Andy to have the following friendly encounter:

ANDY: Oh, well they're friendly ma'am. They're friendly as can be. They're just shy.

ELLEN: Oh, well, I'm glad because that's the one thing I'm looking for is a friendly place. You know, where the people are friendly. Well, I guess you're wondering what I'm doing here in Mayberry. You see, I worked in this big-city barbershop and there was this barber, Pierre, and he was forever after me to marry him and I kept saying I need time to think. You know how a girl needs time to think? Only he didn't think I needed so much time to think, but I did. And well, anyway, we had this big fight and I just had to go away. Well, you could see why I had to do that?

ANDY: Uh, to think.

ELLEN: And besides, I was getting awfully tired of the big city because it's getting so a girl can't walk down the street anymore without being whistled at. Why do men do that?

ANDY: Well, I wouldn't have any idea, would you Floyd?

FLOYD: Oh, no-no-no. I wouldn't know. No-no.

ELLEN: And another thing—the big city isn't a very friendly place—I mean, the people and all. They're not friendly. So, I just decided I'd get on the bus and the first friendly-looking town I came to I'd get off and stay there a while and think things over. And do you know, this bus that I was on, when it came to your city limits, it passed the sign that said, "Welcome to Mayberry, the Friendly Town," and that seemed friendly, so here I am.

ANDY:

Oh, well, we're glad you think we're friendly.

"The Manicurist," Episode 48
Written by Charles Stewart and Jack Elinson

When Henry Bennett thinks he's a jinx with no choice but to leave Mayberry, even after the whole town has tried to rig a raffle in his favor, Andy sets him straight:

ANDY: The way I see it, well,

the luckiest thing a man can have is friendship—

the kind of friendship these folks here tried to show you tonight. With friends like that, I don't hardly see how you can be a loser.

"The Jinx," Episode 49
Written by Jack Elinson and Charles Stewart

Andy and Barney think they want to be members of Raleigh's elite Esquire Club until they both realize that they are already members of the best club in the world:

BARNEY: What's the matter Andy? Why are you looking like that? We're in, aren't we?

ANDY: Well, no. Fact is, they was about to accept one of us.

BARNEY: One of us?

ANDY: Uh-huh.

BARNEY: You must be kidding? I'd like to punch 'em all right in the nose.

ANDY: Now, Barney, there ain't no use to get upset. They got a right to pick who they want, you know.

BARNEY: Of all the nerve, of all the nerve. Boy, this really steams me.

ANDY: Take it easy.

BARNEY: Take it easy nothing. What are they? A bunch of snobs or something?

ANDY: Now, Barney.

BARNEY: Imagine that. Imagine that! Turning down a nice guy like you.

ANDY: Huh?

BARNEY: Who do they think they are, anyway? Boy, they couldn't find a nicer guy than you in the whole world to be in their old club. Well, I'll show 'em.

ANDY: What are you doing?

BARNEY: I'll tell you what I'm doing. **If you ain't good enough for 'em, neither am I.** I'm sending in my resignation.

"The Clubmen," Episode 42
Written by Fred S. Fox and Iz Elinson

Sometimes, the mark of true friendship is just being able to say you're sorry. Take the time that Andy uses his friend Bert Miller as a way to needle stingy department store owner Ben Weaver by setting Bert up with a little curbside vending stand. When Ben fights back with steep price cuts, Andy has to explain things to Bert:

ANDY: Bert, the fact is, you're being squeezed out of business.

BERT: W-what, Andy?

ANDY: Ben Weaver is selling stuff a whole lot cheaper over at his store than you can, so folks are buying from him.

BERT: Oh.

ANDY (observing Bert's humbleness and hurt): Uh, Bert, uh, maybe there's something you oughta know. See, uh, this whole thing started as a joke. Yeah, I was trying to irritate Ben a little bit and, well, I guess it got out of hand.

I'm sorry about that.

"The Merchant of Mayberry," Episode 54
Written by Leo Solomon and Ben Gershman

Strong testimony for a strong friendship:

BARNEY (under oath and on the witness stand): Andy's the best friend I got in the whole world. And as far as I'm concerned he's the best sheriff too. All them things I said—for example his using the squad car for personal reasons—sure, he was delivering groceries to Emma Watson because she was too sick to get down to the market. And that's just one example of the things Andy's done for the folks in this town. I could give you a lot more. You gotta understand this is a small town. The sheriff is more than just a sheriff. He's a friend. And

the people in this town ain't got no better friend than Andy Taylor.

"Andy on Trial," Episode 61
Written by Jack Elinson and Charles Stewart

When Mayor Stoner and Inspector Upchurch don't believe Andy's theory about a thief putting shoes on a cow, they walk out on Andy—with Barney following in their footsteps. But something special makes Barney do an about-face and return:

ANDY: Well?

BARNEY: I just thought I'd wait with you a spell.

ANDY: Well, I appreciate that, Barn. But, the mayor could be right, could be kind of a hare-brained idea.

BARNEY: Well, I'll take my chances. I was almost out to the car and, well, I got to remembering another time a few years back when another mayor of our town accused you of having a hare-brained idea. Remember that? That was when you had the idea of making me your deputy.

"The Cow Thief," Episode 68
Written by R. Allen Saffian (Ray Allen) and Harvey Bullock

Andy and Barney feel nostalgic after an emotion-filled evening of seeing old classmates at their high school reunion:

ANDY: Kinda gets to you a little bit, don't it.

BARNEY: Oh, no. Well, yeah. You know, seeing all those people you knew as kids and growin' older. Kinda makes you sad.

ANDY: Yeah, I know.

Do "the tears on your pillow bespeak the pain? that's in your heart".

BARNEY: Yeah.

ANDY: Me too.

"Class Reunion," Episode 82
Written by Everett Greenbaum and Jim Fritzell

When you're friends, sometimes you have to be willing to accept a little egg on your faces when something has been said or heard that seems a little too hardboiled:

ANDY: I'm surprised at you, a gentleman's gentleman, running out on a promise.

MALCOLM: Well, I did leave you a note, sir. You see, I thought ...

ANDY: I don't know what you thought or what you heard. **Fact is, it's a terrible thing—the high sheriff having to tie his own tie. Worst of all, Opie's back there having to eat eggs without faces on 'em. You call that living correctly?**

MALCOLM: Oh, no sir.

ANDY: You better turn around and get right back to work.

MALCOLM: Yes, sir, right away. I'll turn to it directly.

ANDY: You see to it. Fact is,

I want the whole lot to be a regular bobby dazzler.

"Andy's English Valet," Episode 89
Written by Harvey Bullock

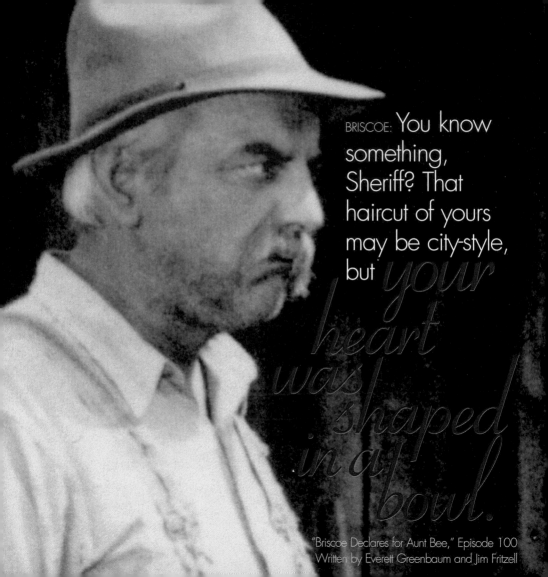

BRISCOE: You know something, Sheriff? That haircut of yours may be city-style, but *your heart was shaped in a bowl.*

"Briscoe Declares for Aunt Bee," Episode 100
Written by Everett Greenbaum and Jim Fritzell

After Andy and Barney have saved Mrs. Mendelbright from being swindled by a false suitor, Barney and Mrs. Mendelbright, helped along by cider that has turned hard, share how they feel about each other:

BARNEY:
I should have taken better care of you.

You're my friend.

MRS. MENDELBRIGHT: Oh, Barney, you're my friend, too.

BARNEY: I like you, Mrs. Mendelbright.

MRS. MENDELBRIGHT: I like you, too, Barney.

"Up in Barney's Room," Episode 105
Written by Jim Fritzell and Everett Greenbaum

OPIE: Are we poor?

   ANDY: No, we're not poor. I'd say we're better off than a lot of people. Got a roof over our heads, Aunt Bee, the finest food you ever put in your mouth. Barney for a friend. Yeah, in some ways I'd say we *are* rich.

BARNEY: You see, Ope, it ain't only the materialistic things in this world that makes a person rich. There's love and friendship. *That* can make a person rich.

   AUNT BEE: Very nicely put, Barney.

ANDY: I don't believe I ever heard that said any better.

BARNEY: Yes sir, Ope, it ain't only the materialistic things in this world that makes a person rich. You know what else does? Love and friendship.

ANDY: That's right.

BARNEY: I bet you thought it was only the materialistic things, huh? Well, it ain't.

ANDY: **There's love and friendship.**

"Opie and His Merry Men," Episode 107
Written by John Whedon

After Opie and his new pal Trey leave the Courthouse as bosom buddies, Andy and Barney are prompted to reflect on their own friendship:

BARNEY: You know it's the friendships you start early in life—them are the ones that really last.

ANDY: Hmm.

BARNEY: Take you and me now. How long have we been hanging together? Since fourth grade.

    ANDY: 4-A.

BARNEY: Yeah. Miss Moran.

    ANDY: Oh, Miss Moran. Bless her heart. Well, time's jumping right along, Barn.

BARNEY: Yeah, well, that's what makes friendship so good—the test of time. I couldn't wish them two boys anything better than that they should become as close of friends as you and me.

After having a quarrel, Opie and his buddy Trey seem to have realized the same thing about friendship, as Opie discusses the matter with Andy that evening at home:

OPIE: Pa, Trey and me—we're friends again.

    ANDY: Good, I'm glad to hear it.

OPIE: You think Barney'll make up too?

    ANDY: Aw, sure he will.

OPIE: And we can all go fishing tomorrow. Trey can use your pole and wear Barney's hat.

    ANDY: Good. We'll call Trey first thing in the morning.

OPIE: We don't have to.

    ANDY: What do you mean?

OPIE: Well, come here.

(Opie takes Andy to his bedroom where Trey is asleep in his bed snuggled up to a football.)

OPIE: I gave it to him to keep. He told me this was the first time he's ever had a genuine, full-size, regulation football.

    ANDY: He's got something even better than that, son.

Now he's got a genuine, full-size, regulation friend to match. In fact, we all have. "Andy and Opie's Pal," Episode 109
Written by Harvey Bullock

BARNEY: You know, Andy, take a tip from a guy that's been around. **When two friends, especially when it's a man and a woman that are having a fight, just don't get involved.** It won't work. Am I getting through to you, fella?

"Man in the Middle," Episode 134
Written by Gus Adrian
and David Evans

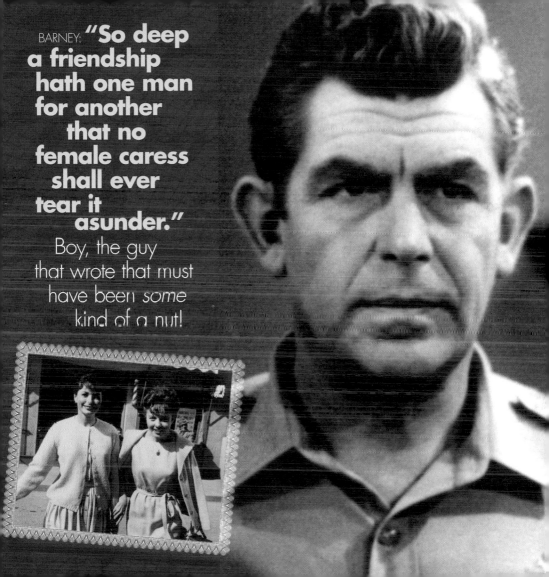

BARNEY: **"So deep a friendship hath one man for another that no female caress shall ever tear it asunder."** Boy, the guy that wrote that must have been *some* kind of a nut!

When it looks as if Otis is going to start choosing Mt. Pilot as his permanent place to turn himself in on weekends, Andy and Barney realize just how much they'll miss their old friend, flaws and all:

BARNEY: I don't mind telling you—I miss him. I really miss him.

ANDY: Well, I do too, I guess.

BARNEY (holding up Otis's bathrobe): What do you think we ought to do with this? Box it up and send it to him in Mt. Pilot?

ANDY: Well, I guess we could.

BARNEY: Good color for Otis. He always looked good in blue. You know, Andy, Otis had a lot of problems and he's weak in a lot of ways, but well, we've known him for a good many years and **it's just kind of sad when you realize that we're not going to be seeing** *this old friend.*

"The Rehabilitation of Otis," Episode 145
Written by Lawrence J. Cohen and Fred Freeman

Every once in a while, two good friends need another friend to remind them what good friends they really are:

ANDY: Maybe now we can settle this thing like friends.

CHARLIE FOLEY: Friends, huh? Do friends punch you in the nose?

FLOYD: Do friends call you a crook?

CHARLIE: Well you *are* a crook.

(Foley and Floyd argue.)

ANDY: Wait a minute! Now let's not start the whole thing all over again. You've both known one another much too long to talk to each other like that. Now I mean it! You've been friends for twenty years. More than friends, you've been neighbors. You must've seen one another through a lot of trouble in that time. Now, you're not kids, either one of you. And you both know the value of old friends.

And the first law of friendship
is to be ready to forgive.

"The Case of the Punch in the Nose," Episode 152
Written by Bill Idelson and Sam Bobrick

Feeling that you have something important in common, like, say,
being Irish, can be a powerful bond for some friendships:

ERNEST T. BASS: Malcolm, I ain't gonna touch a hair on your head. You're my friend, my true friend. I don't care if you did take my job away from me and ruin my matrimonial chances with my beloved Romeena.

You're my friend, Malcolm, my bosom pal. I love you, I love you, I loooove you!

"Malcolm at the Crossroads," Episode 162
Written by Harvey Bullock

Andy and Barney are waiting in the courthouse for the newspaperman to come over after Barney has captured an escaped criminal during Barney's visit to Mayberry:

BARNEY: Is Farley coming over?

ANDY: Are you kidding? This is front-page stuff.

BARNEY: Yeah. Listen, when you talk to him, kind of swing the credit to Warren for the capture there, will you?

ANDY: Swing the credit to Warren? He wasn't even close by.

BARNEY: Yeah, I know, but

sometimes it don't hurt to shade things a little when you want to help somebody.

ANDY: Yeah, I suppose.

BARNEY: After all, Ange, I've had my place in the sun here for a lot of years. Now a nice fellow like that comes along. A little pat on the back'll make him feel good. It's his town out there now, Andy. It's not mine. I'll see if Farley's coming.

(Barney and Warren pass each other at the doorway.)

WARREN: A true living legend that Barney Fife. I mean, he's something isn't he, Andy?

ANDY: Yes, he is. He really is.

"The Legend of Barney Fife," Episode 177
Written by Harvey Bullock

As Andy knocks five times on the door to the Regal Order of the Golden Door to Good Fellowship, Goober comes out to man the entrance:

ANDY: You the keeper of the door?

GOOBER: Yeah, this month.

(He holds up a golden key.)

ANDY: Request permission to enter the Golden Door to Good Fellowship.

GOOBER: Qualify yourself to enter the Golden Door.

ANDY (whispering): Geronimo.

GOOBER: What?

ANDY (a little louder, but still secretively): Geronimo.

GOOBER:

Enter in the name of good fellowship.

"The Lodge," Episode 191
Written by Jim Parker and Arnold Margolin

Though Howard Sprague had caught elusive fish Old Sam a few days earlier, Floyd and Goober are debating whether Floyd just saw Old Sam swimming by in Tucker's Lake as Opie and Howard approach along the shoreline:

GOOBER: That *was* Old Sam then! I knew it, I knew it!

FLOYD: How come you decided to put him back?

HOWARD: You know, Opie and I went up to the aquarium in Raleigh, and, well, we were standing by the tank there and Old Sam came right over to the glass of the tank—right where we were standing—and started moving his mouth.

GOOBER: Moving his mouth?

HOWARD: Yeah. Well, we stood there watching him for a while and we finally figured out what he was trying to say.

FLOYD: He was trying to *talk*?

HOWARD: Yeah. He was trying to tell us,

"Gosh, would I like to see Goober and Floyd and Andy and everybody again."

So, well, after that, I just had to put him back.

FLOYD: Ah-hah, that's the greatest thing I ever heard.

Fish may or may not talk, but one thing's for sure: It's the ultimate act of friendship to let your friends—and their dreams—swim free.

"Big Fish in a Small Town," Episode 200
Written by Bill Idelson and Sam Bobrick

Aunt Bee and Clara share homemade cookies on the Taylors' front porch after Clara has insisted that Aunt Bee's damaged rose win the flower contest based solely on a photo taken of the rose before it was damaged:

AUNT BEE: That was a very nice thing you did, Clara.

CLARA: Oh, but when I saw that picture of your rose . . .

AUNT BEE: I know but you had the contest won and you let me have it.

CLARA: No, no. There was no doubt but that yours was a superior flower.

AUNT BEE: Well, it's still a very nice thing for you to do.

CLARA: Well, what are friends for? And you would have won it.

AUNT BEE: Well, you'll win it next year. And let's not let a silly contest make us quarrel again.

CLARA: We never will.

We've been friends for so long.

"Only a Rose," Episode 201
Written by Jim Parker and Arnold Margolin

When Goober grows a beard and suddenly thinks that he knows everything, he starts to get under the skin of even his best friends. But it's hard to confront a friend with a beard who has so many thoughts to share about the nature of friendship itself:

FLOYD: Goober, there comes a time when a friend has to tell a friend something. You follow me?

GOOBER: Well, sure. If a friend can't tell a friend something, then nobody can tell him nothing.

FLOYD: Yes.

GOOBER: 'Cause when a friend talks to you, you don't listen with your ears. You listen with your heart.

FLOYD: Well, what I wanted to say to you…we listen…ohhh, what a lovely thought.

GOOBER: It just come to me.

FLOYD: Had a nice ring to it.

GOOBER: You know something else it brings to mind about friends?

FLOYD: What?

GOOBER: That even sometimes these great philosophers can be wrong.

FLOYD: They can?

GOOBER: Uh-huh.

A man's best friend is not his dog.
It's people.

FLOYD: Ohhh, you really get to the meat of things, Goober. Go on.

GOOBER: 'Course, I still love dogs.

"Goober Makes History," Episode 203
Written by Paul David and John L. Greene

When Goober forgets to tell Andy that he has been invited to dinner at the Spragues' house until after Andy has already finished the spaghetti dinner Goober made for him, Andy remains pretty friendly and polite with Goober:

ANDY (to Goober): Howard Sprague is a very close friend of mine, so…

I've been invited to dinner, and I better show up. THANKS!

GOOBER: You're welcome.

A maxim to store in the old noodle: The difference between remaining a friend and becoming a foe apparently lies somewhere between having a second and a third spaghetti dinner:

ANDY (to Goober): Now I'm going over to Helen's and eat my third supper and then I'm coming back…

and I'm gonna kill you.

"Dinner at Eight," Episode 206
Written by Budd Grossman

Howard Sprague moves to the Caribbean in search of the good life, but he returns to Mayberry:

ANDY: I thought you wanted to follow your rainbow and everything.

HOWARD: Yeah, well, I guess I just followed it to the wrong end.

My pot of gold's right here in Mayberry.

"Howard's New Life," Episode 234
Written by Dick Bensfield and Perry Grant

Opie makes a banana split for his pal Arnold:

ARNOLD: More syrup.

OPIE: That's all we give.

ARNOLD: I'm your friend.

OPIE: **Look, Arnold, I can't give every friend who comes in here more than he's supposed to get.** Now we want your business, Arnold, but this stuff costs money. How is it?

ARNOLD: Not bad. You make a pretty good banana split for a kid.

OPIE: Thanks.

"Opie's Drugstore Job," Episode 238
Written by Kent Wilson

Even after his old pal Roy Swanson has taken delight in catching Goober putting on airs, Goober refuses to go into that same greasepit of spite when he finds that Roy too has been exaggerating his success:

ANDY: Wanna say hello to an old friend?

GOOBER: No, no, it might embarrass him. I wouldn't want to do that.

ANDY: Goob, I wouldn't worry any more about trying to be a big man.

GOOBER: Why not?

ANDY: *You made it.*

"Goober Goes to an Auto Show," Episode 241
Written by Joseph Bonaduce

Andy gives a toast to Mayberry at Thelma Lou and Barney's wedding reception:

There's something about Mayberry and
Mayberry folk that never leaves you.
No matter where life takes you,
you always carry in your heart the
memories of old times…
and old friends. *Here's to old friends.*

Return to Mayberry
Written by Everett Greenbaum and Harvey Bullock

Lots of Luck to *you* and *yours!*